THE SOUND OF MUSIC

Broadway Souvenir Folio Edition

Featuring scenes from the 1998 Broadway production

Do-Re-Mi. Rebecca Luker with (left to right): Ashley Rose Orr, Andrea Bowen, Tracy Alison Walsh, Matthew Ballinger, Natalie Hall, Ryan Hopkins, Sara Zelle

Production photos by Joan Marcus

Applications for performance of this work, whether legitimate, stock, amateur or foreign, should be addressed to:

THE RODGERS & HAMMERSTEIN THEATRE LIBRARY
229 West 28th Street, 11th floor • New York, NY 10001
Phone: (212) 564-4000
Fax: (212) 268-1245

ISBN 0-7935-9876-1

WILLIAMSON MUSIC
A RODGERS AND HAMMERSTEIN COMPANY
www.williamsonmusic.com

EXCLUSIVELY DISTRIBUTED BY

HAL•LEONARD CORPORATION
7777 W. BLUEMOUND RD. P.O. BOX 13819 MILWAUKEE, WI 53213

Williamson Music is a registered trademark of the Rodgers Family Partnership and the Estate of Oscar Hammerstein II.

CONTENTS

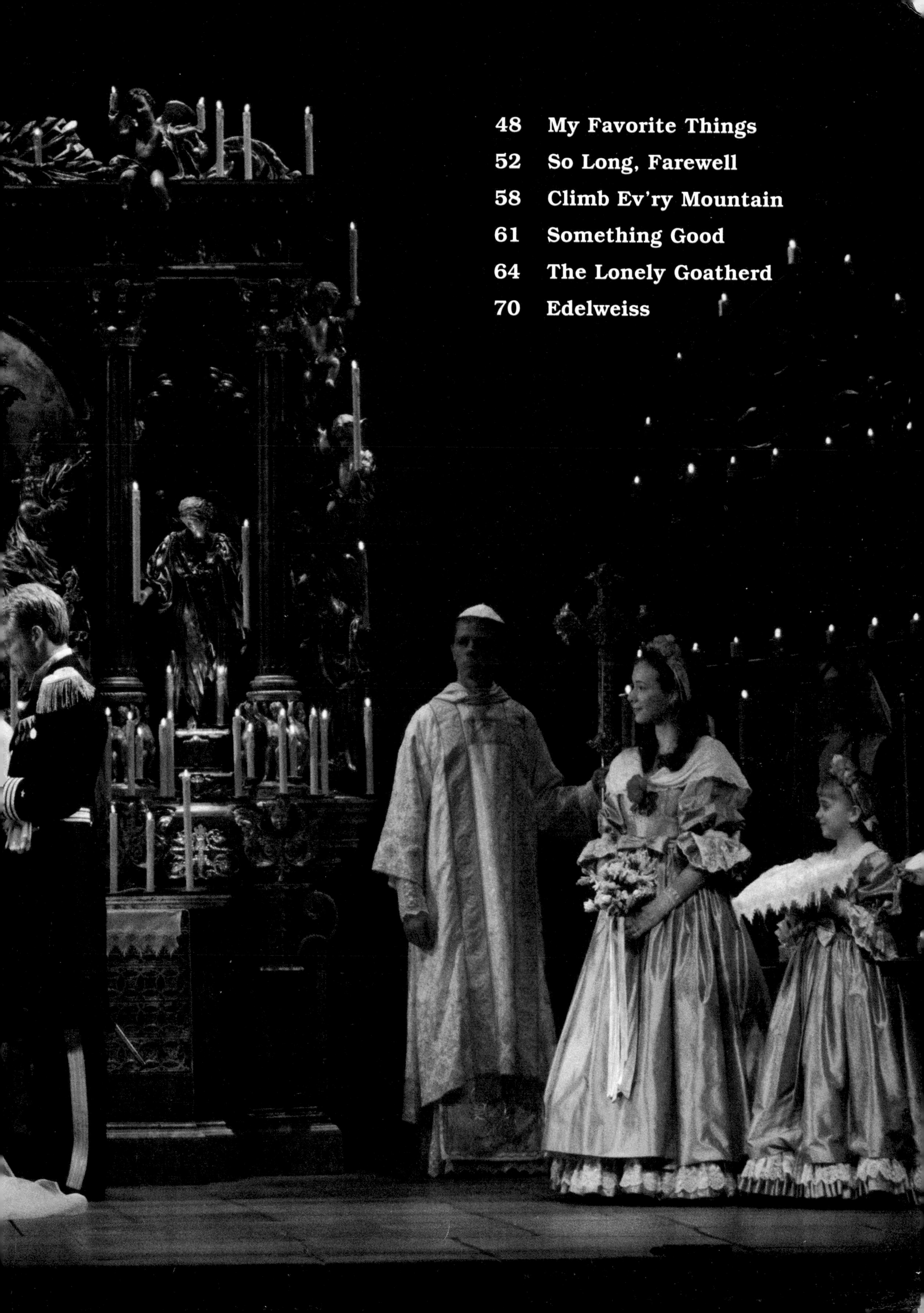

The Sound of Music. Rebecca Luker

Maria. (left to right) Gina Ferrall, Ann Brown, Jeanne Lehman and Patti Cohenour

I Have Confidence. Rebecca Luker

Do-Re-Mi. (left to right) Ashley Rose Orr, Andrea Bowen, Tracy Alison Walsh, Matthew Ballinger, Natalie Hall, Ryan Hopkins, Sara Zelle and Rebecca Luker

Sixteen Going on Seventeen. Sara Zelle and Dashiell Eaves

My Favorite Things. (clockwise from left) Sara Zelle, Natalie Hall, Rebecca Luker, Matthew Ballinger, Andrea Bowen, Ryan Hopkins, Tracy Alison Walsh and Ashley Rose Orr

So Long, Farewell. (clockwise from left) Natalie Hall, Ryan Hopkins, Andrea Bowen, Sara Zelle, Matthew Ballinger, Tracy Alison Walsh and Ashley Rose Orr

Climb Ev'ry Mountain. Patti Cohenour

The Lonely Goatherd. The Family von Trapp: Rebecca Luker, Michael Siberry and children

Something Good. Michael Siberry and Rebecca Luker

Edelweiss. Michael Siberry

"With Songs They Have Sung, For a Thousand Years"

By Theodore S. Chapin

"It seems improbable that there is any living soul who doesn't know the story of *The Sound of Music*." So wrote Mary Martin in 1976, seventeen years after she starred in the original production. In fact, *The Sound of Music* was created for her, and she had the clout to pull in the best writers imaginable: Richard Rodgers, Oscar Hammerstein II, Howard Lindsay and Russel Crouse. As they provided her with a Tony Award-winning role in a Tony Award-winning show (it won eight in all), they created what is arguably the most beloved musical of all time. Critics have found things to gripe about, but *The Sound of Music* has simply ignored them throughout its history—as both a stage musical and as a film—and found audience after audience, year after year. The show continues to hold some remarkable records, including the longest run of an American musical in London, and a film version that remains in the Top 10 on *Variety*'s list of all-time box-office champs. What Mary Martin felt improbable in 1976 remains close to impossible today. *The Sound of Music* has simply become part of world culture.

So how do you approach a show that is so indelibly etched on everyone's soul, in which every song seems like an old friend? The collaborators on the 1998 Broadway production began, logically, with the script of the original production. It provided some surprises — Max and Elsa, for instance, whose roles were minimized in the film version. They are very real characters with very strong (and political) points of view. And the script revealed more of an edge than was expected; the threat of the *Anschluss* is more pointed and focused. Then director Susan H. Schulman and set designer Heidi Ettinger made a trip to the actual locations where the story took place, in search of authenticity. The ever-present mountains of Salzburg (even mid-morning coffee in someone's home is served out on a terrace) inspired Ettinger's fluid and painterly scenery, brilliantly lit by Paul Gallo. Many of Catherine Zuber's colorful costumes used fabric acquired from shops in Salzburg that had been in business since the 1930's — you can't get more authentic than that! Schulman and Ettinger's visit to Nonnberg Abbey revealed much about the daily life behind those cloistered walls. They were also able to speak with one nun who had been in the Abbey with the real-life Maria. Bringing all this research to the table has made this production different in feel from both the original and the film, and allowed it to find a modern reality for the Broadway of today.

At the heart of the show is, of course, its score. Individually these songs have become so well-known and loved through the years that one could easily assume they had started life as a collection of popular favorites. Eight songs from the original show are standards: "The Sound of Music," "My Favorite Things," "Do-Re-Mi," "Sixteen Going on Seventeen," "The Lonely Goatherd," "So Long, Farewell," "Climb Ev'ry Mountain," and "Edelweiss." The two orchestral pieces, "Laendler" and "The Wedding Processional," are staples of the concert world, and the two songs created for the movie, "I Have Confidence" and "Something Good," have become standards as well. No other Broadway score can match those statistics. And it is all the more remarkable when you discover that the show was written within one six-month period in 1959.

The writers of *The Sound of Music* (left to right): composer Richard Rodgers, lyricist Oscar Hammerstein II, and book writers Howard Lindsay and Russel Crouse.
(Photo courtesy of The Rodgers and Hammerstein Organization)

Familiar though the songs may be, they are clearly born of the theater. Rodgers and Hammerstein were extraordinary on a number of levels, not the least of which was their ability to operate as songwriters and dramatists at the same time. Every song in *The Sound of Music* was written with characters and situations in mind. "Do-Re-Mi" is about teaching children, but it's done in musical terms because Maria wants to bring music back into a household from which it had been removed. "So Long, Farewell" is ostensibly about children going off to bed, but it is used to cover the two most important exits in the show: when Maria decides to leave the von Trapp house and return to the Abbey, and as the von Trapp family flees their beloved Austria at the end. "Sixteen Going on Seventeen" is a song of innocent teenage romance, but since Rolf and Liesl are about to be thrust into some very adult situations beyond their control, they use words to show they are grown up: "roués and cads," "bachelor dandies," etc. "The Lonely Goatherd" passes by with the innocence of a child's song, yet its story of a man and woman who find each other through singing (yodeling, to be exact) is an interesting reflection on the main plot. It is also an indication of the genius of Rodgers and Hammerstein how the series of clever "...-oat heard" rhymes are musically downplayed in favor of the robust, beer-stein-clinking, yodeling melody.

And how these songs have entered the collective consciousness of the world! Can we ever hear the line "brown paper packages tied up with strings" and not think of the melody that goes with it? How many Marias have walked down the aisle to "The Wedding Processional?" (Shriver, for one, since she had a call placed to our office to ask permission!) And surely the Italian music theorist who invented the simple group of one-syllable words assigned to each note of the diatonic scale would have been pleased — if a little perplexed — by the immortality his invention achieved with "Do-Re-Mi." And an absurd level of achievement was reached when, assuming "Edelweiss" to be an authentic Austrian folk song, the Ronald Reagan White House had the Navy band play it at a dinner in honor of a visiting Austrian dignitary.

It is a testament to Rodgers and Hammerstein that a body of songs written to tell a specific theatrical story has moved so many people for so long; like songs we have sung "for a thousand years," they are almost folksong-like in their familiarity.

"Let's Start at the Very Beginning..."
A Look at the World's Most Beloved Musical

By Bert Fink

In 1958, Mary Martin, the eternally youthful star of *South Pacific* and *Peter Pan*, was involved in an exciting new project: she and husband-producer Richard Halliday began working with the distinguished playwrighting team of Howard Lindsay and Russel Crouse to create a stage play about the von Trapp family. The play, based on a German film called *Die Trapp Familie*, would tell the true-life story of how the Austrian von Trapps fled their homeland following the Nazi *Anschluss* on the eve of World War II and found haven in America as a singing troupe.

Mary Martin as Maria in a scene from the original 1959 Broadway production of *The Sound of Music*.
(Photo courtesy of The Rodgers and Hammerstein Organization)

Of course, even in a play Mary Martin would want to sing, so Lindsay & Crouse planned their script to include a sampling of the religious and folk songs the von Trapps had actually sung. Along the way, Martin's good friends Richard Rodgers and Oscar Hammerstein II were asked to write a song especially for her to sing in this new play, too.

R&H loved working with Mary Martin, but had a better idea: why not let them write an entirely new score for this story—as a musical? That is, if the team already in place would be willing to wait a year since R&H were already working on *Flower Drum Song*. The flattering—and wise—decision from Martin, Halliday, Lindsay, Crouse and co-producer Leland Hayward: "We'll wait." Rodgers & Hammerstein started crafting the score in March of 1959. Rehearsals began in August, the world premiere occurred in New Haven in October, and Broadway had a new musical hit by November.

With a $5 top ticket price, *The Sound of Music* boasted an advance sale of over $2 million ($30 million by today's standards). Audiences adored Martin and took the musical to their hearts. It ran for 1,443 performances and earned eight Tony Awards, including Best Musical. The original cast album earned a Gold Record and a Grammy Award.

In 1961, with the musical still going strong on Broadway, a U.S. National Tour was launched, starring Florence Henderson. That same year saw the start of a marathon run at London's Palace Theatre, where *The Sound of Music* still holds the record as the longest-running American musical in the West End.

And then there is... The Movie. Winner of five Academy Awards, including Best Picture, *The Sound of Music* has become the most popular movie musical ever made and has also triumphed on television and home video.

More than a hit show or cultural phenomenon, *The Sound of Music* is a rarity that has touched the hearts of its audiences since the very beginning. Evidently, it meant a great deal to the four men who wrote it, too. Rodgers seemed to speak for them all when, in a letter to Lindsay's wife Dorothy years later, he called *The Sound of Music* "one of the happiest experiences of my theatrical life."

Thomas Viertel • Steven Baruch • Richard Frankel • Jujamcyn Theaters

in association with

The Rodgers and Hammerstein Organization • Charles Kelman Productions

Simone Genatt Haft • Marc Routh • Jay Binder • Robert Halmi, Jr.

present

Rebecca Luker

Michael Siberry

in

THE SOUND OF MUSIC

Music by	Lyrics by		Book by
Richard Rodgers	**Oscar Hammerstein II**	**Howard Lindsay**	**Russel Crouse**

Suggested by "The Trapp Family Singers" by Maria Augusta Trapp

also starring

Patti Cohenour

with

Jan Maxwell   Fred Applegate

Patricia Conolly   Sara Zelle   Dashiell Eaves   John Curless

Ryan Hopkins   Natalie Hall   Matthew Ballinger   Tracy Alison Walsh   Andrea Bowen   Ashley Rose Orr

Jeanne Lehman   Gina Ferrall   Ann Brown   Timothy Landfield   Reno Roop   Gannon McHale

Anne Allgood   Joan Barber   Laura Benanti   Nora Blackall   Marissa Gould   Martha Hawley
Kelly Cae Hogan   Siri Howard   Tad Ingram   Matt Loney   Betsi Morrison
Patricia Phillips   Lynn C. Pinto   Lou Taylor Pucci   Kristie Dale Sanders   Margaret Shafer   Ben Sheaffer

Scenery by	Costumes by	Lighting by
Heidi Ettinger	**Catherine Zuber**	**Paul Gallo**

Sound Design	Wigs and Hair Design	Casting
Tony Meola	**Paul Huntley**	**Jay Binder**

Orchestrations by	Dance and Incidental Music Arrangements	Original Orchestrations by	Original Choral and Dance Arrangements	Music Coordinator
Bruce Coughlin	**Jeanine Tesori**	**Robert Russell Bennett**	**Trude Rittmann**	**John Miller**

Production Manager	Production Supervisor	General Management	Press Representative	Associate Producers
Peter Fulbright	**Beverley Randolph**	**Richard Frankel Productions Laura Green**	**Peter Cromarty & Company**	**James D. Stern PACE Theatrical Group**

Music Direction by

Michael Rafter

Choreography by

Michael Lichtefeld

Directed by

Susan H. Schulman

The New Broadway Cast Recording On RCA Victor

THE SOUND OF MUSIC

Lyrics by OSCAR HAMMERSTEIN II
Music by RICHARD RODGERS

My day in the hills has come to an end, I know. A star has come out to tell me it's time to go. But deep in the dark green shad - ows are

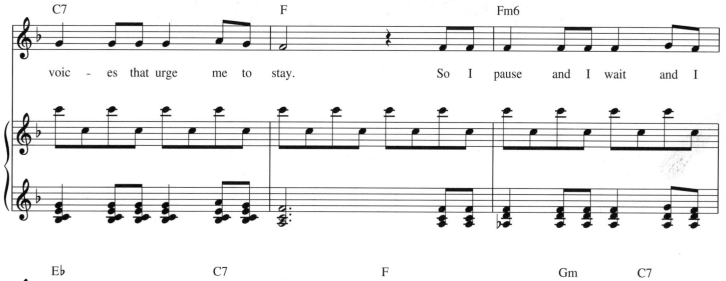

voic - es that urge me to stay. So I pause and I wait and I

lis - ten for one more sound, For one more love-ly thing that the hills might

rit.

Refrain *(moderately, with warm expression)*

say. The hills are a-live with the sound of mu - sic, _____

più rit. *p a tempo*

_____ With songs they have sung for a thou - sand years. _____

The hills fill my heart with the sound of mu - sic.

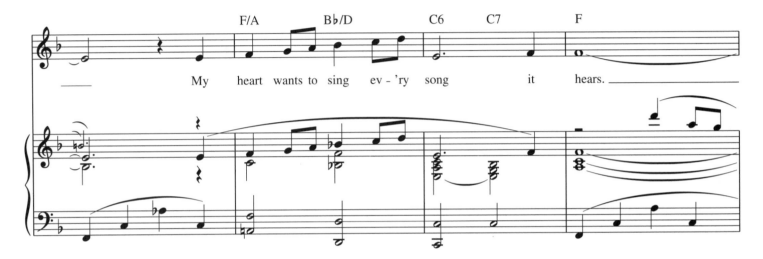

My heart wants to sing ev - 'ry song it hears.

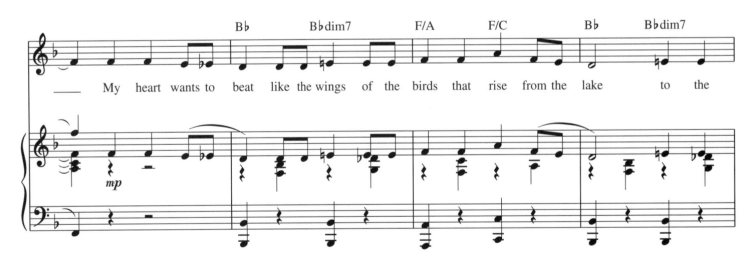

My heart wants to beat like the wings of the birds that rise from the lake to the

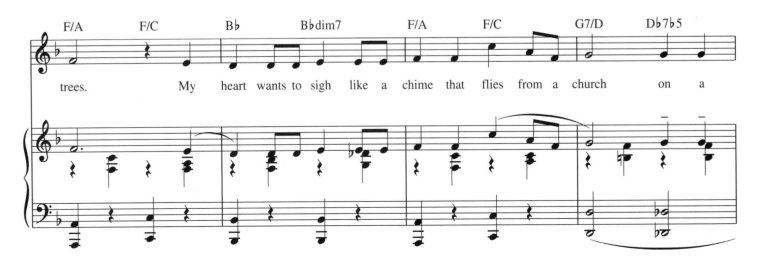

trees. My heart wants to sigh like a chime that flies from a church on a

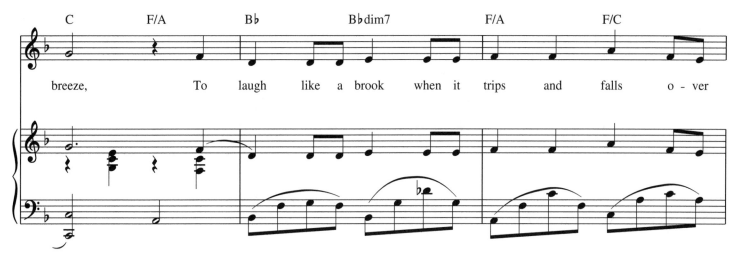

breeze, To laugh like a brook when it trips and falls o - ver

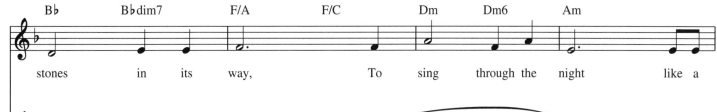

stones in its way, To sing through the night like a

lark who is learn - ing to pray. I go to the hills

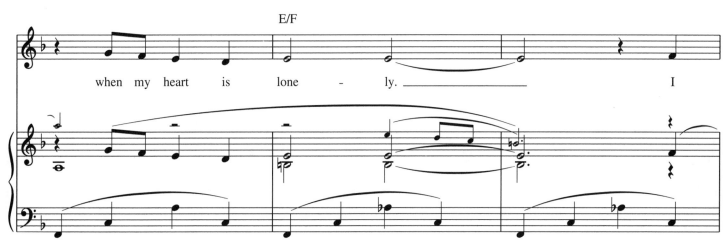

when my heart is lone - ly. I

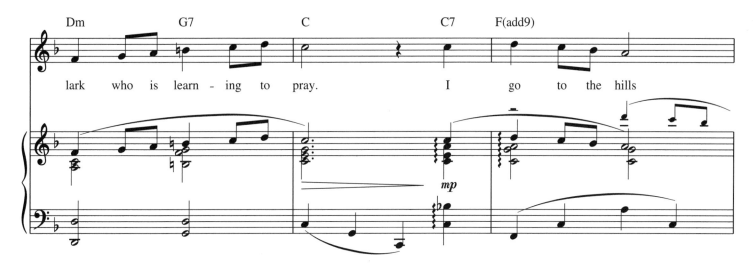

know I will hear what I've heard be - fore.

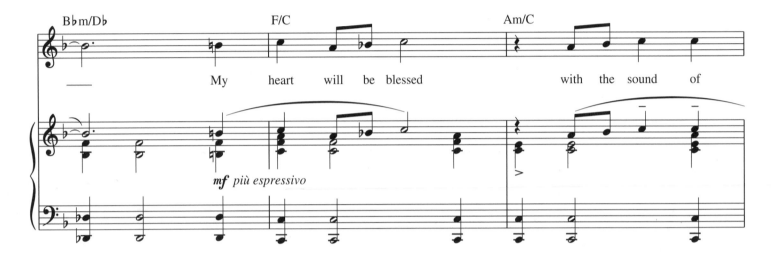

My heart will be blessed with the sound of

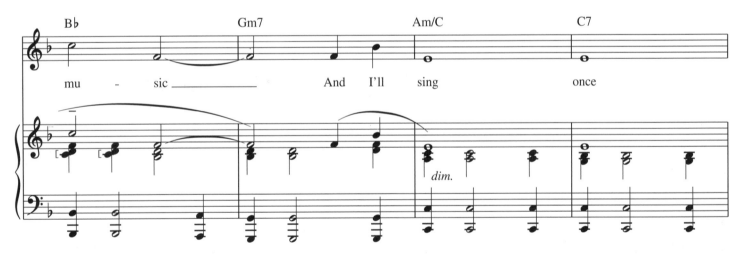

mu - sic And I'll sing once

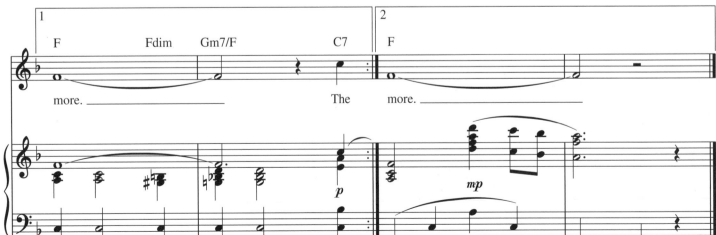

more. The more.

MARIA

Lyrics by OSCAR HAMMERSTEIN II
Music by RICHARD RODGERS

Allegretto con moto

BERTHE: She climbs a tree and scrapes her knee, Her dress has got a tear. _____ **SOPHIA:** She waltz-es on her way to mass and whis-tles on the stair. _____ **BERTHE:** And un-der-neath her wim-ple she has curl-ers in her hair. _____ **SOPHIA:** Ma-

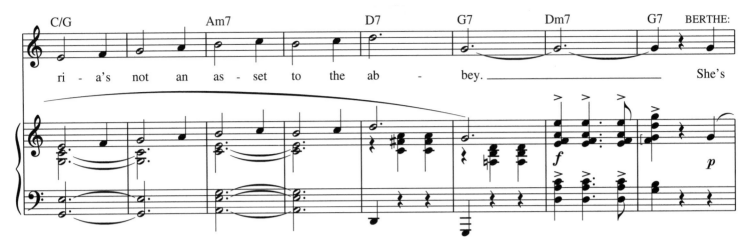

ri - a's not an as - set to the ab - bey. _____ She's

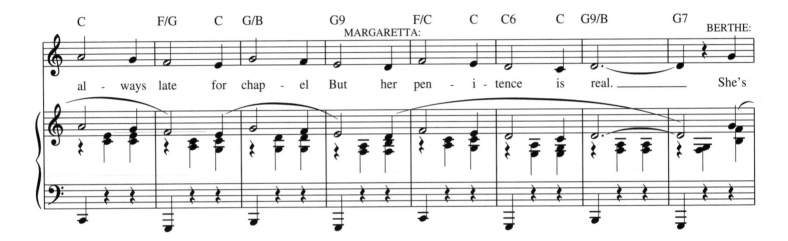

al - ways late for chap - el But her pen - i - tence is real. _____ She's

MARGARETTA:

BERTHE:

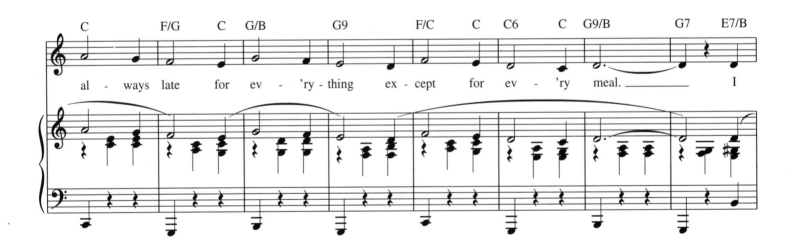

al - ways late for ev - 'ry - thing ex - cept for ev - 'ry meal. _____ I

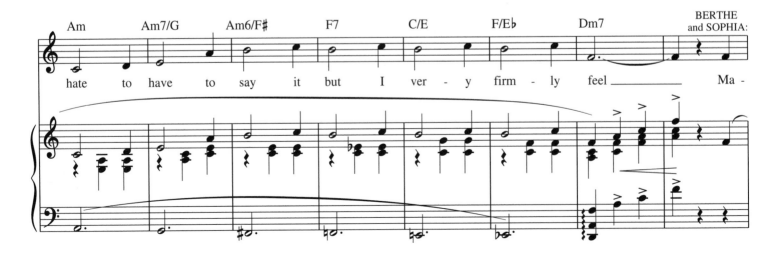

hate to have to say it but I ver - y firm - ly feel _____ Ma -

BERTHE and SOPHIA:

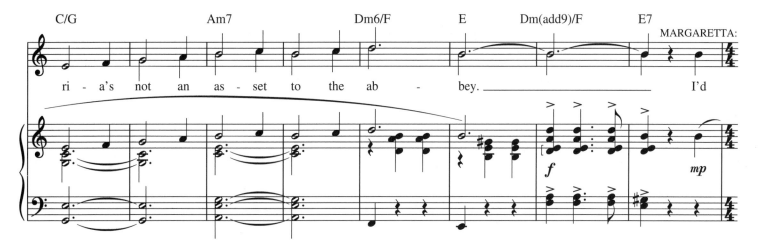

C/G　　Am7　　Dm6/F　E　Dm(add9)/F　E7

MARGARETTA:

ri - a's not an as - set to the ab - bey. _____ I'd

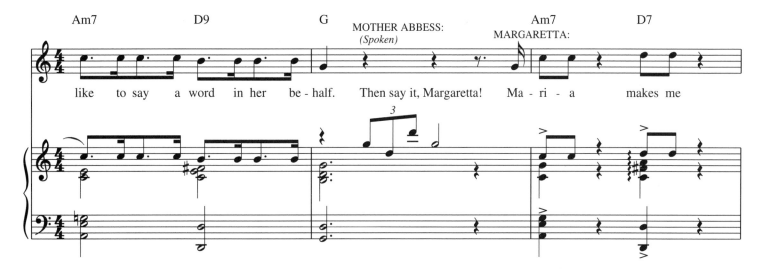

Am7　　D9　　G

MOTHER ABBESS: *(Spoken)*
MARGARETTA:
Am7　　D7

like to say a word in her be - half. Then say it, Margaretta! Ma - ri - a makes me

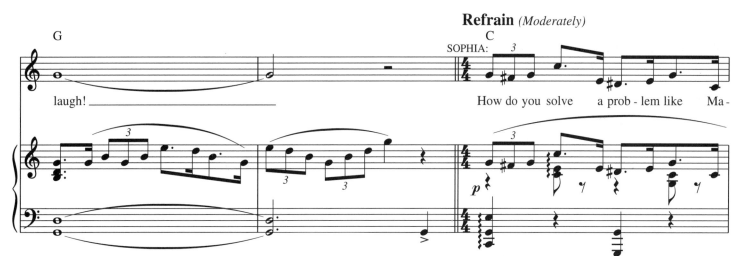

G

Refrain *(Moderately)*
C

SOPHIA:

laugh! _____ How do you solve a prob - lem like Ma -

G7　　C　　G

MOTHER ABBESS:

ri - a? How do you catch a cloud and pin it down?

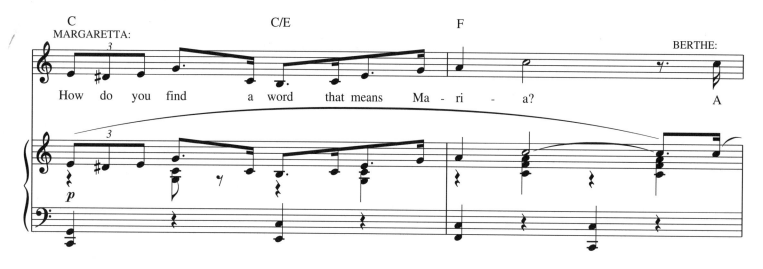

MARGARETTA: How do you find a word that means Ma-ri-a?

BERTHE: A

SOPHIA: flib-ber-ti-gib-bet! A will-o' the wisp!

MARGARETTA: A clown!

MOTHER ABBESS: Man-y a thing you know you'd like to tell her;

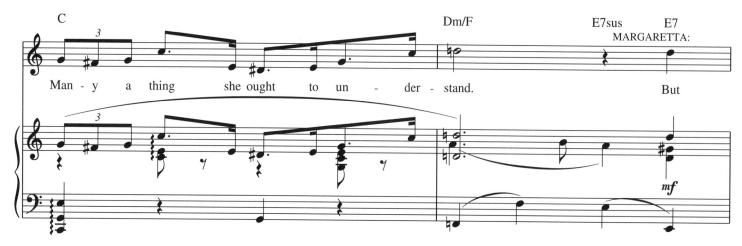

Man-y a thing she ought to un-der-stand.

MARGARETTA: But

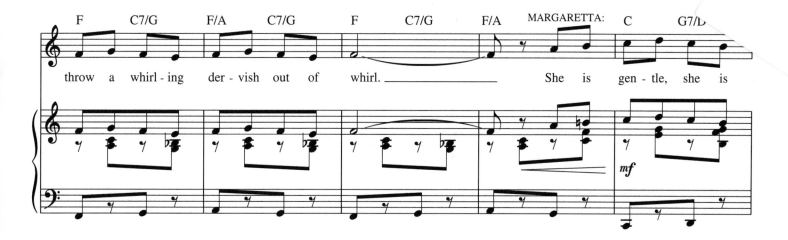

throw a whirl-ing der-vish out of whirl. _____ She is gen-tle, she is

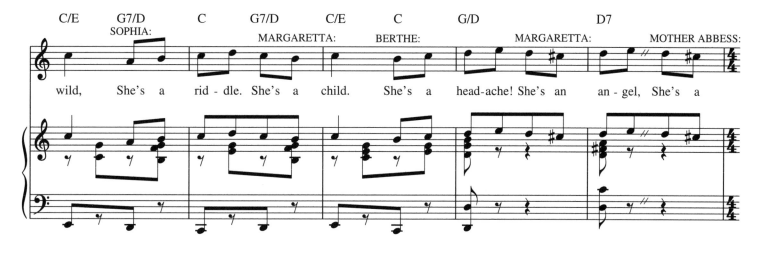

wild, She's a rid-dle. She's a child. She's a head-ache! She's an an-gel, She's a

Tempo I

girl. _____ How do you solve a prob-lem like Ma-

ri - a? How do you catch a cloud and pin it down?

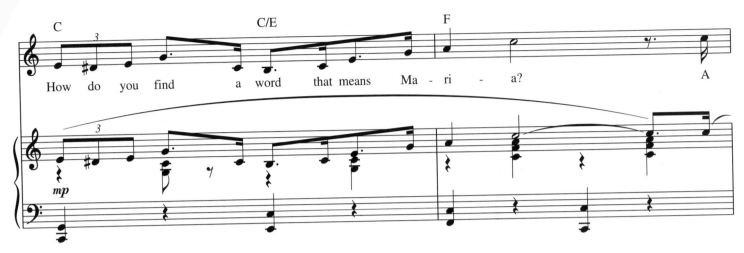

How do you find a word that means Ma-ri - a?

A

flib - ber - ti - gib - bet! A will - o' the wisp! A clown!

Man - y a thing you know you'd like to tell her;

Man - y a thing she ought to un - der - stand.

But

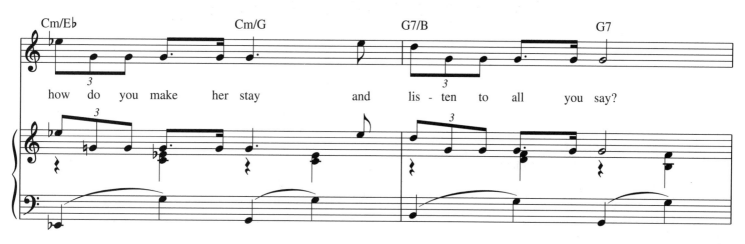

how do you make her stay and lis - ten to all you say?

How do you keep a wave up - on the sand? Oh,

how do you solve a prob - lem like Ma - ri - a? How do you hold a

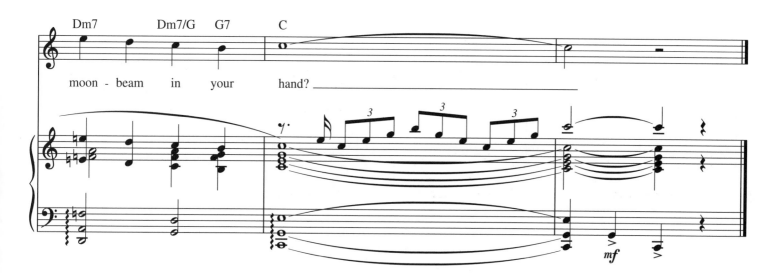

moon - beam in your hand?

I HAVE CONFIDENCE

Lyrics and Music by
RICHARD RODGERS

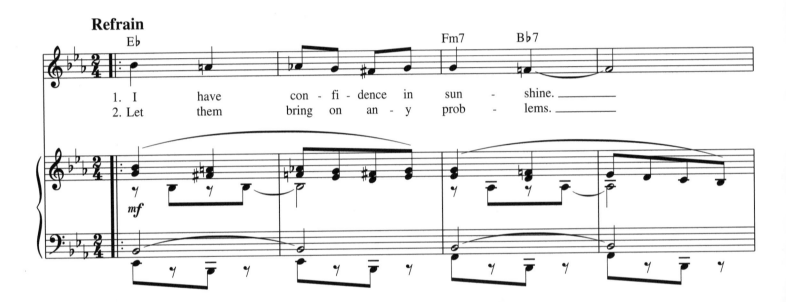

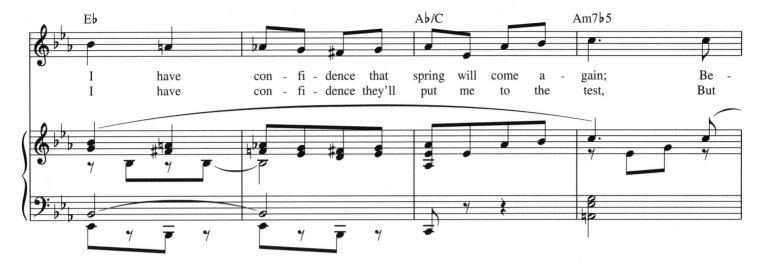

I have con - fi - dence that spring will come a - gain; Be -
I have con - fi - dence they'll put me to the test, But

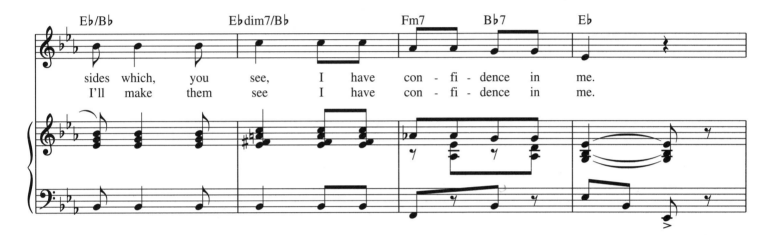

sides which, you see, I have con - fi - dence in me.
I'll make them see I have con - fi - dence in me.

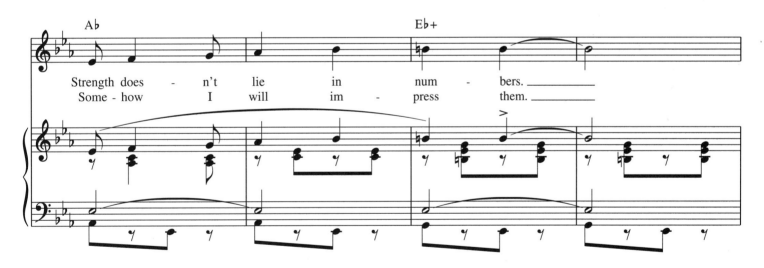

Strength does - n't lie in num - bers. _____
Some - how I will im - press them. _____

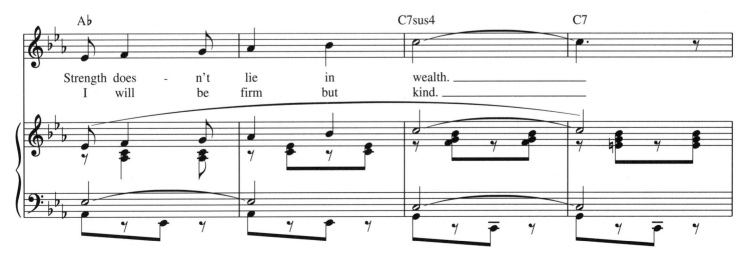

Strength does - n't lie in wealth. _____
I will be firm but kind. _____

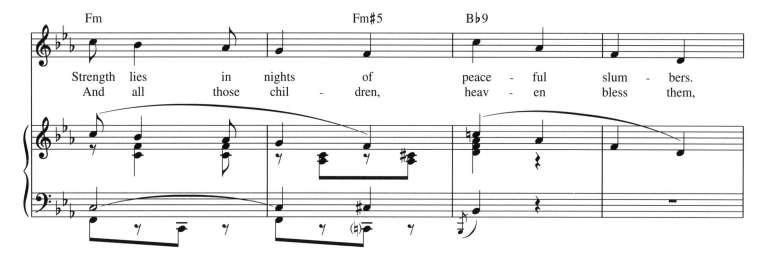

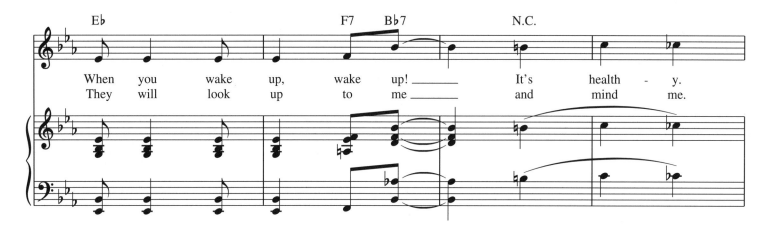

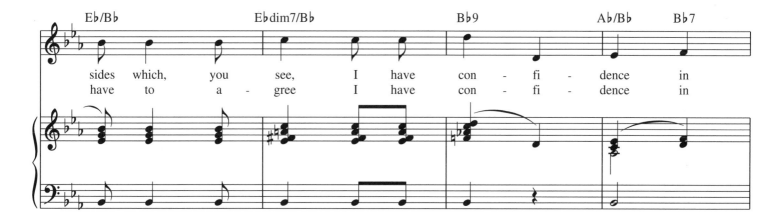

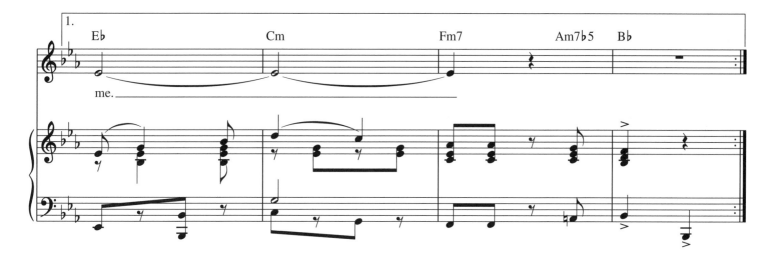

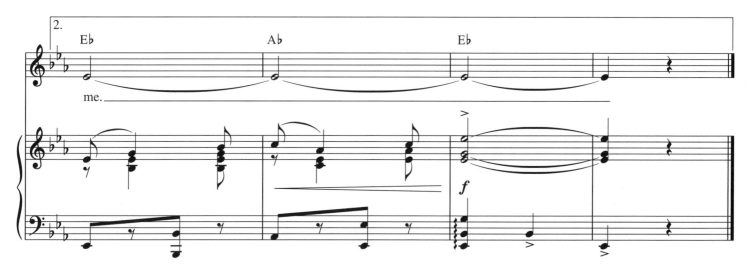

DO-RE-MI

Lyrics by OSCAR HAMMERSTEIN II
Music by RICHARD RODGERS

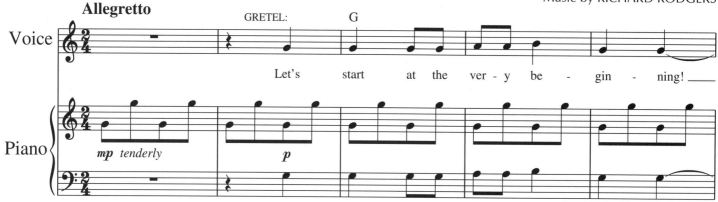

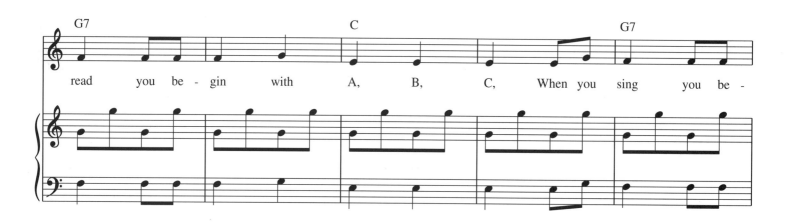

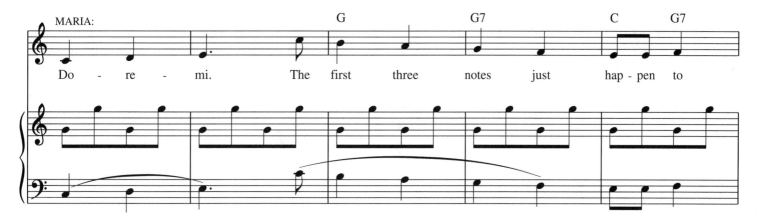

MARIA:

Do - re - mi. The first three notes just hap-pen to

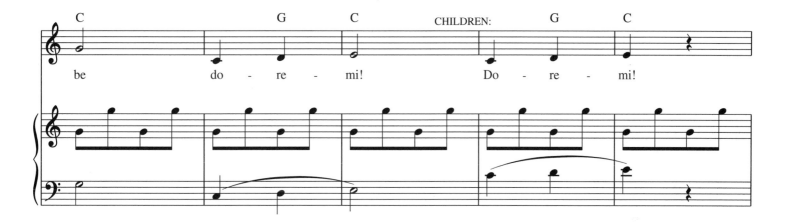

be do - re - mi! CHILDREN: Do - re - mi!

MARIA:

Do - re - mi - fa - so - la - ti ___ (Spoken) All right, I'll make it easier. Listen:

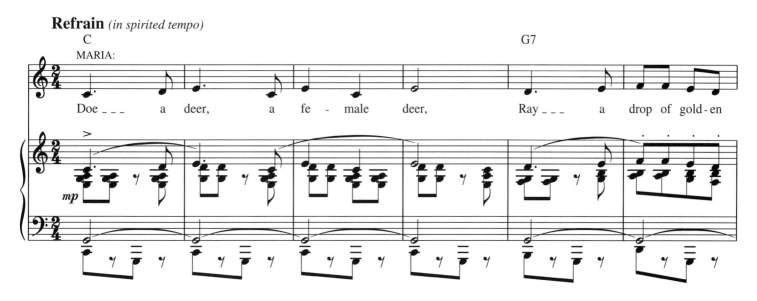

Refrain *(in spirited tempo)*

MARIA:

Doe ___ a deer, a fe - male deer, Ray ___ a drop of gold - en

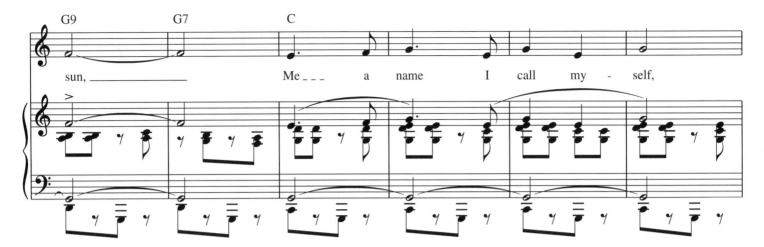

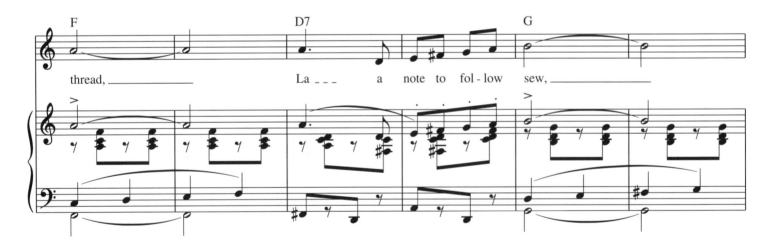

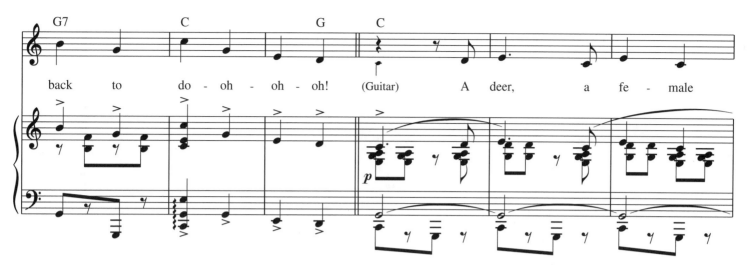

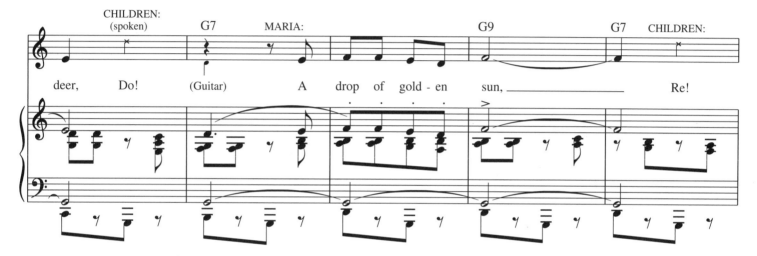

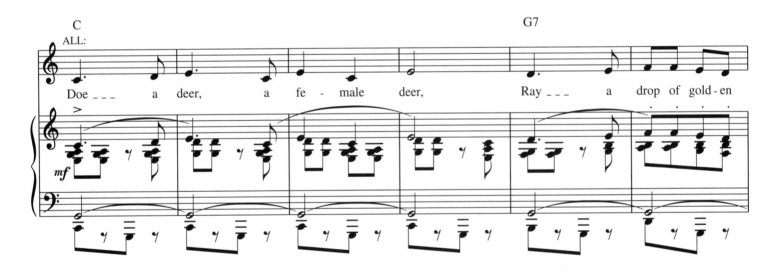

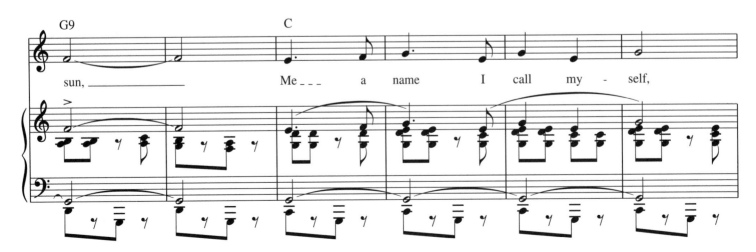

Far ___ a long, long way to run. _____ Sew ___ a nee - dle pull - ing

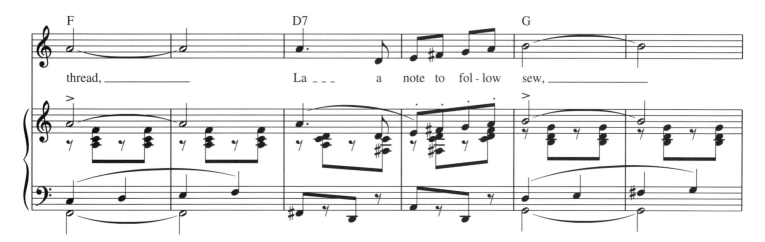

thread, _____ La ___ a note to fol - low sew, _____

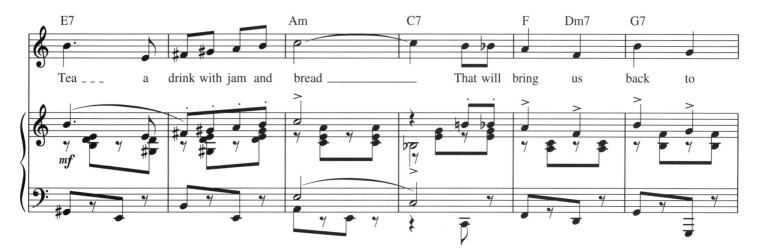

Tea ___ a drink with jam and bread _____ That will bring us back to

doe! _____ Do - re - mi - fa - so - la - ti - do! _____

SIXTEEN GOING ON SEVENTEEN

Lyrics by OSCAR HAMMERSTEIN II
Music by RICHARD RODGERS

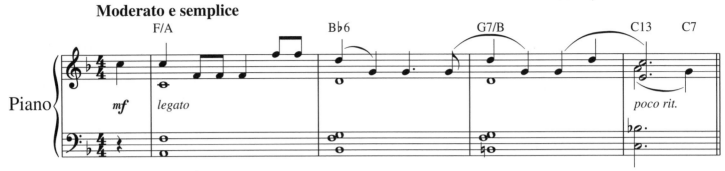

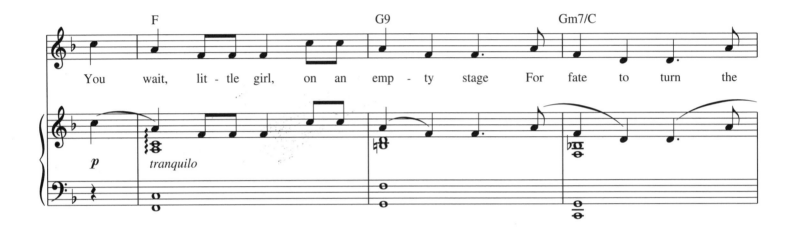

You wait, lit-tle girl, on an emp-ty stage For fate to turn the

light on. Your life, lit-tle girl, is an emp-ty page That

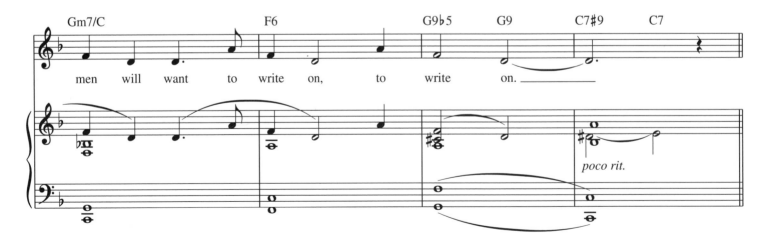

men will want to write on, to write on. _____

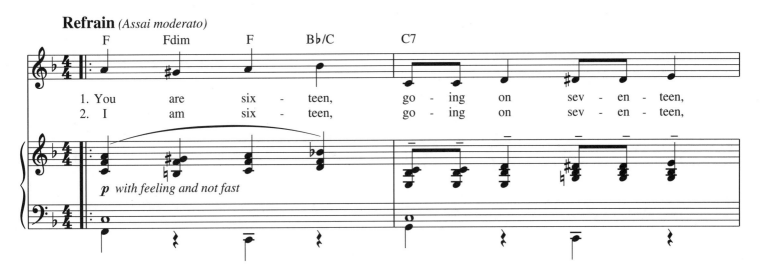

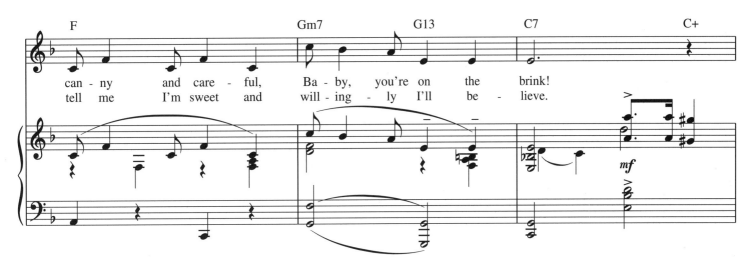

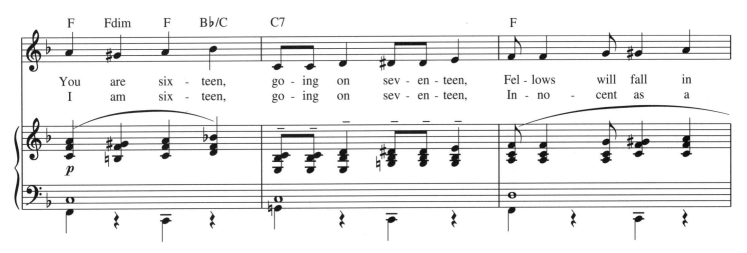

Refrain *(Assai moderato)*

1. You are six - teen, go - ing on sev - en - teen,
2. I am six - teen, go - ing on sev - en - teen,

Ba - by, it's time to think! Bet - ter be - ware, be
I know that I'm na - ive. Fel - lows I meet may

can - ny and care - ful, Ba - by, you're on the brink!
tell me I'm sweet and will - ing - ly I'll be - lieve.

You are six - teen, go - ing on sev - en - teen, Fel - lows will fall in a
I am six - teen, go - ing on sev - en - teen, In - no - cent as a

p with feeling and not fast

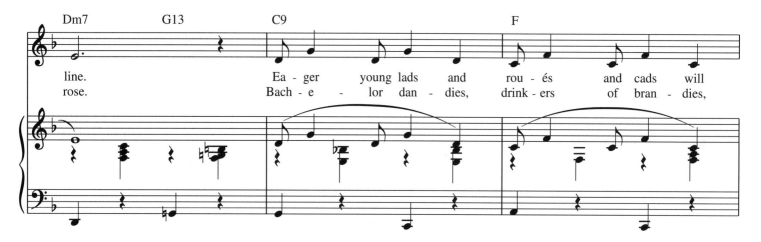

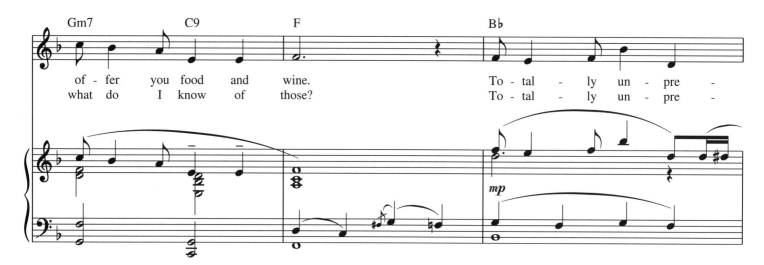

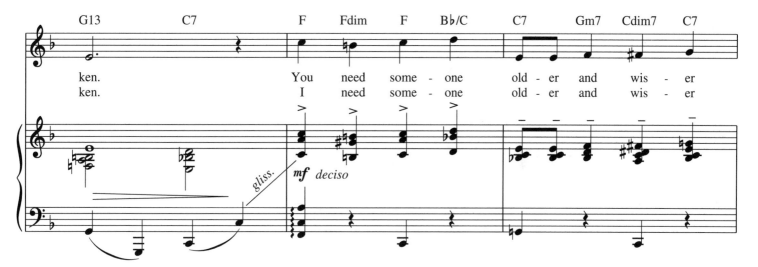

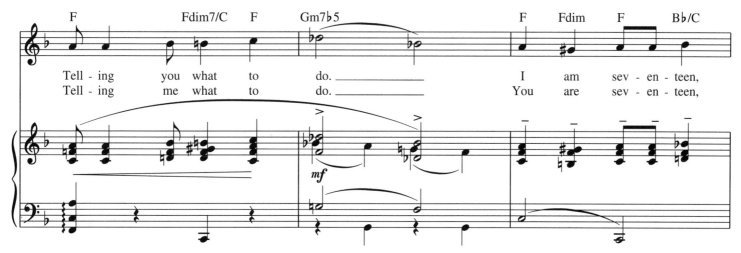

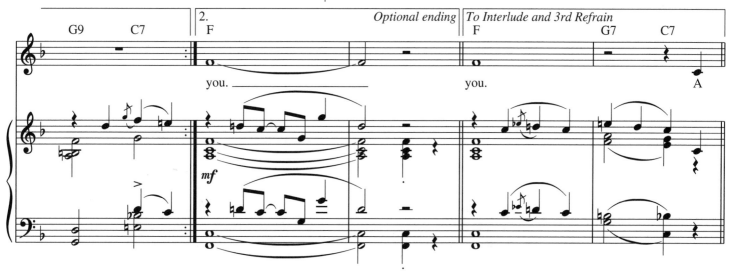

44

Interlude

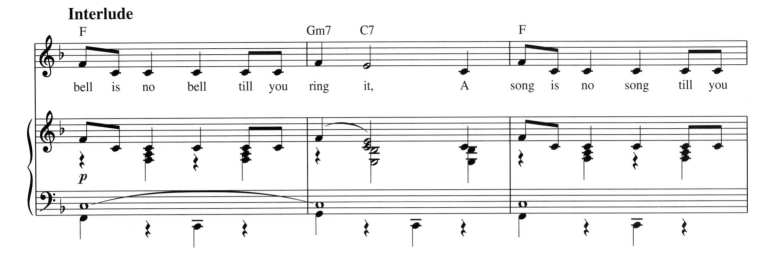

bell is no bell till you ring it, A song is no song till you

sing it, And love in your heart was -n't

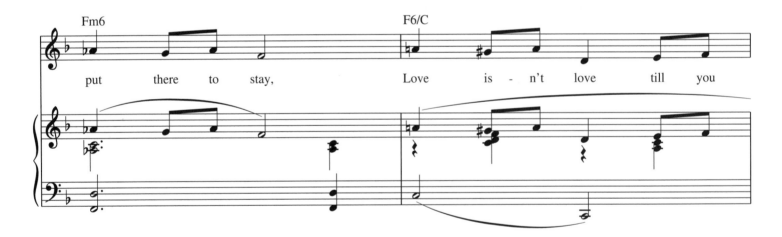

put there to stay, Love is -n't love till you

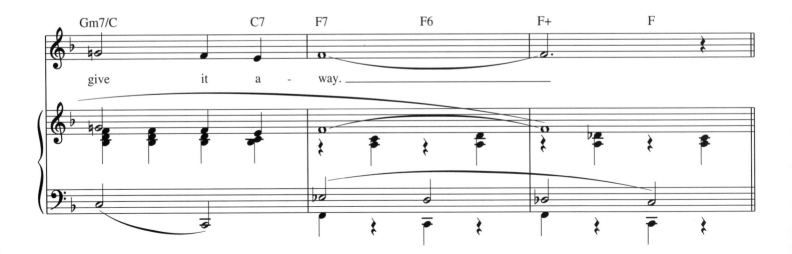

give it a - way.

3rd Refrain *(Assai moderato)*

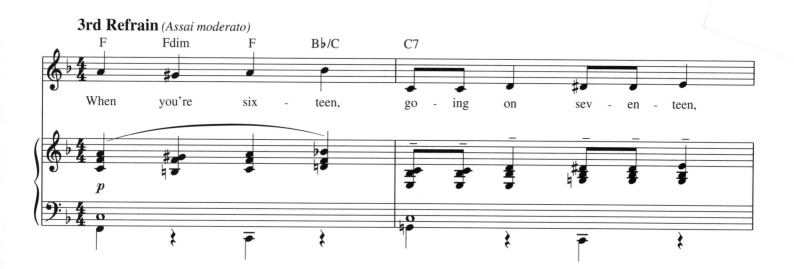

When you're six - teen, go - ing on sev - en - teen,

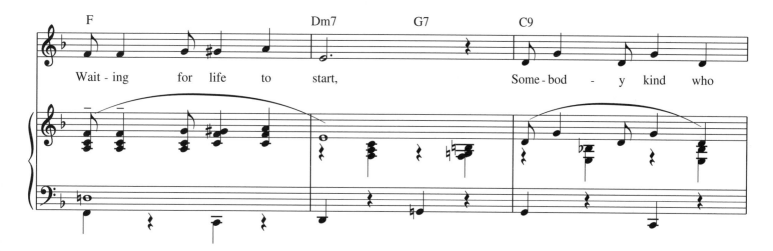

Wait - ing for life to start, Some - bod - y kind who

touch - es your mind will sud - den - ly touch your heart!

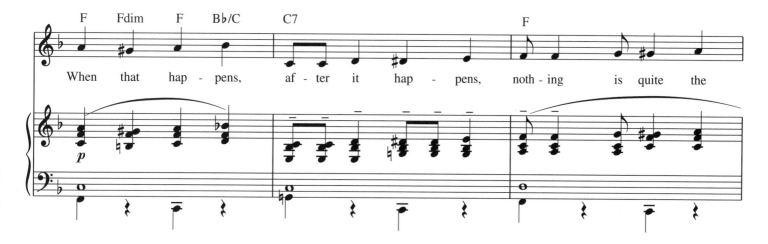

When that hap - pens, af - ter it hap - pens, noth - ing is quite the

46

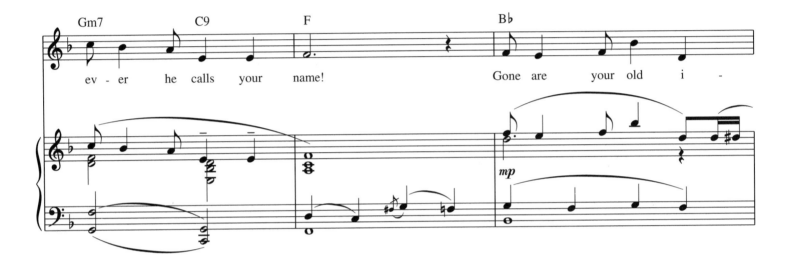

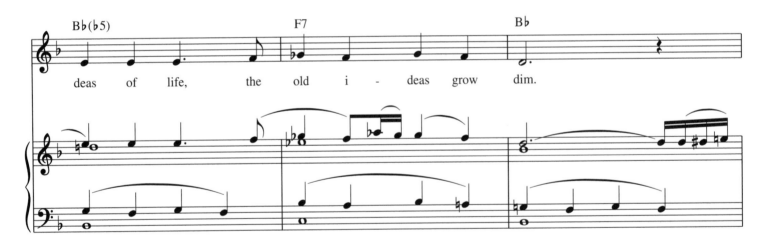

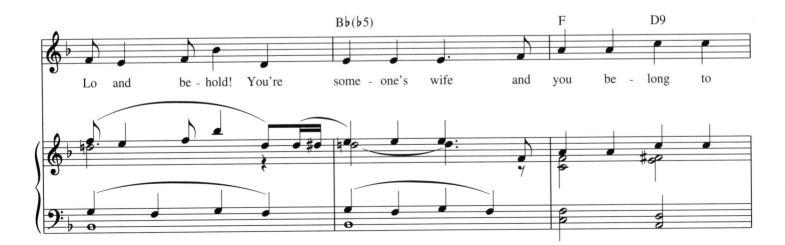

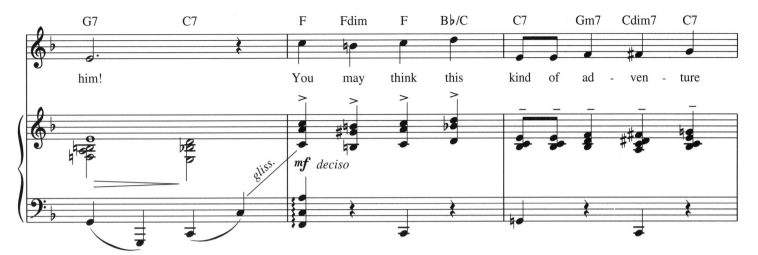

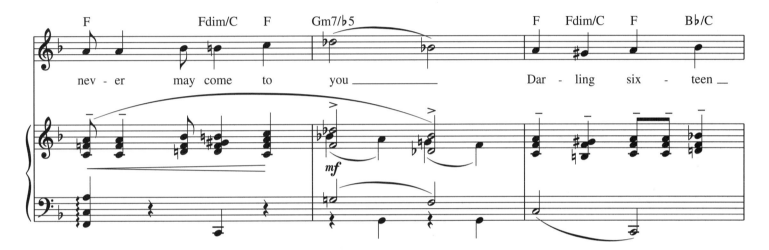

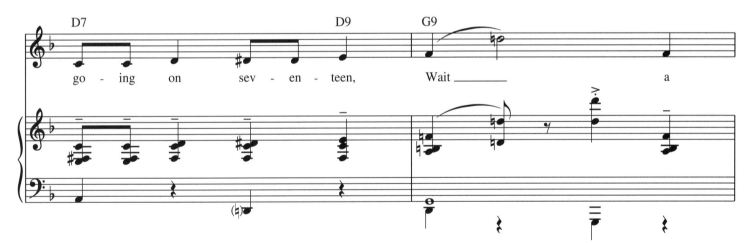

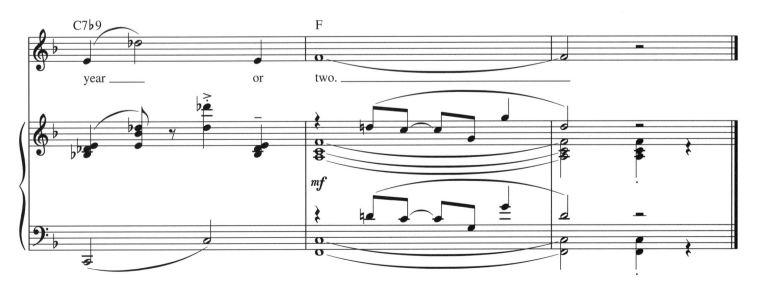

MY FAVORITE THINGS

Lyrics by OSCAR HAMMERSTEIN II
Music by RICHARD RODGERS

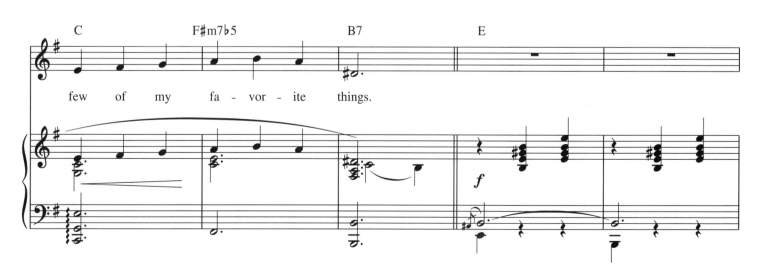

Girls in white dress - es with blue sat - in sash - es, Snow - flakes that

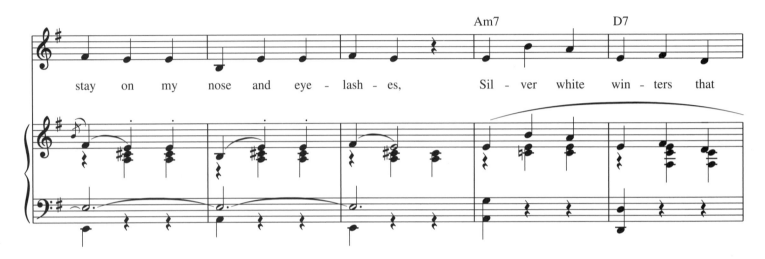

stay on my nose and eye - lash - es, Sil - ver white win - ters that

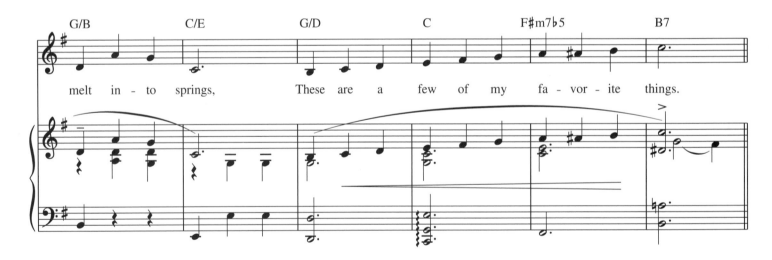

melt in - to springs, These are a few of my fa - vor - ite things.

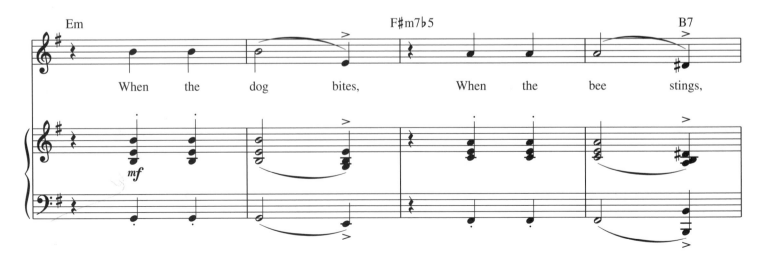

When the dog bites, When the bee stings,

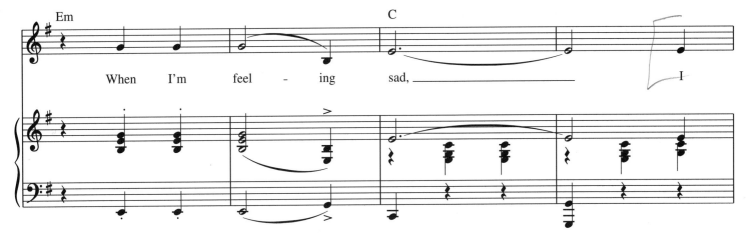

When I'm feel - ing sad, _____ I

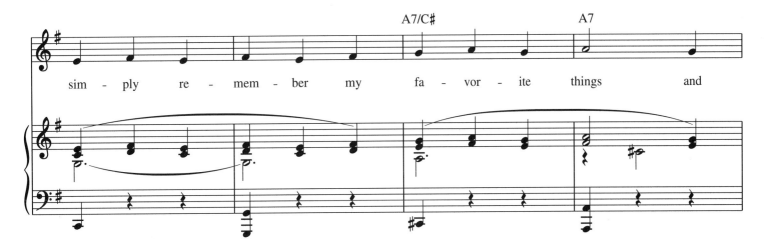

sim - ply re - mem - ber my fa - vor - ite things and

then I don't feel so bad. _____

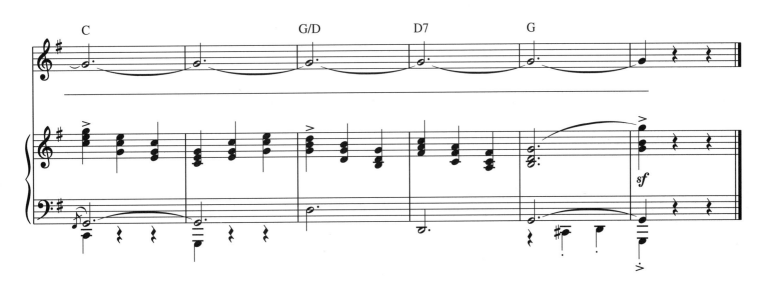

SO LONG, FAREWELL

Lyrics by OSCAR HAMMERSTEIN II
Music by RICHARD RODGERS

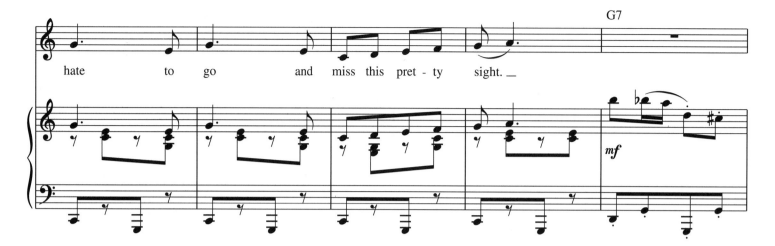

hate to go and miss this pret - ty sight. __

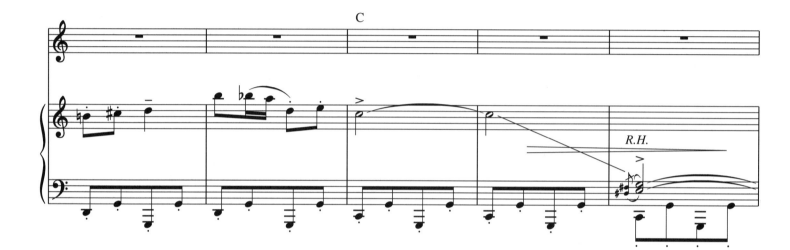

CHILDREN: KURT:

So long, fare - well, Auf wie - der - sehn, a - dieu, __ a -

dieu, A - dieu, to yieu and yieu and yieu. __

C

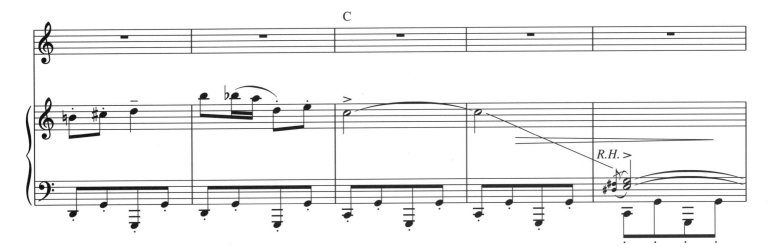

CHILDREN: LIESL:

So   long,   fare - well,   Au' - voir, Auf wie - der - sehn, __   I'd

G7

like   to stay   and taste my first cham - pagne. __

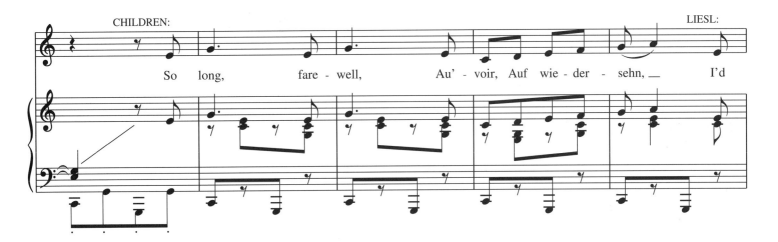

C

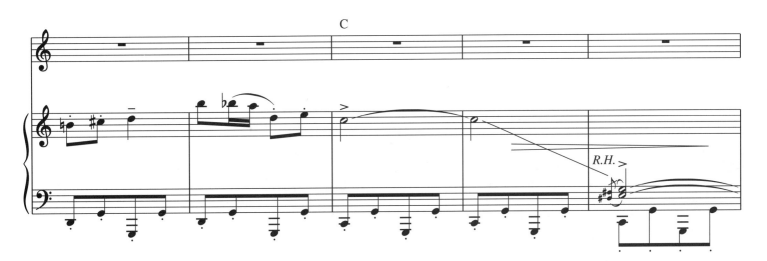

fleet - ly flee, I fly. ___

Molto tranquillo

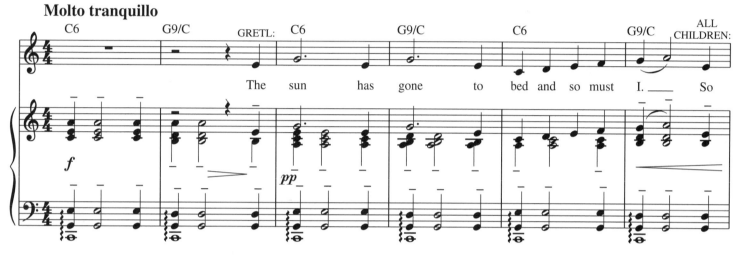

The sun has gone to bed and so must I. ___ So

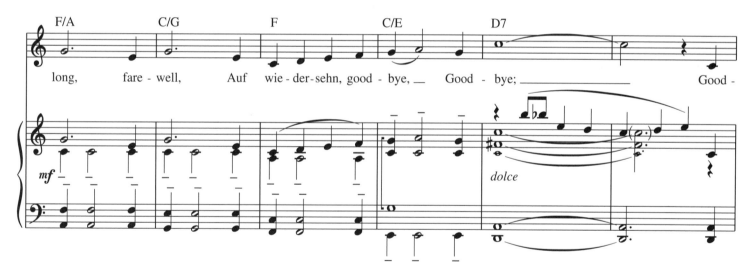

long, fare - well, Auf wie - der - sehn, good - bye, __ Good - bye; _____ Good -

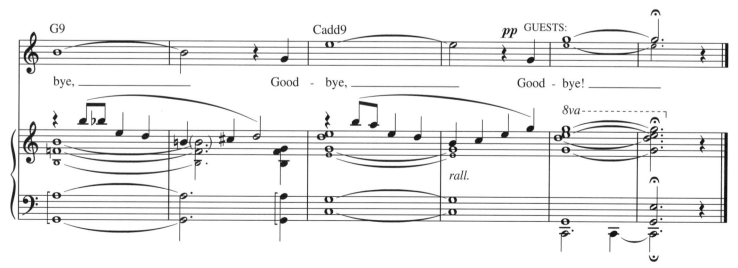

bye, _____ Good - bye, _____ Good - bye! _____

CLIMB EV'RY MOUNTAIN

Lyrics by OSCAR HAMMERSTEIN II
Music by RICHARD RODGERS

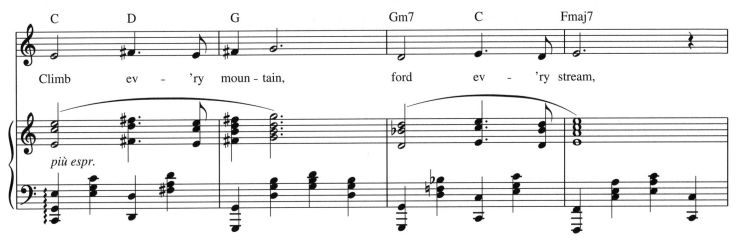

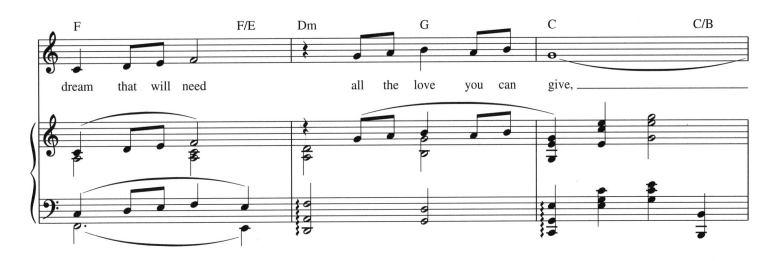

Allargando

live. _____ Climb ev - 'ry moun - tain,

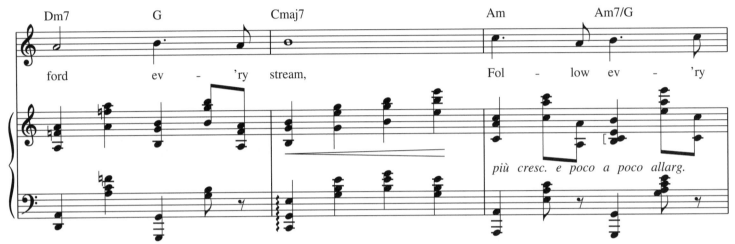

ford ev - 'ry stream, Fol - low ev - 'ry

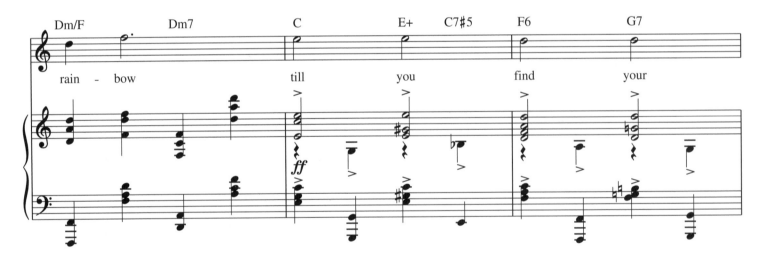

rain - bow till you find your

dream! dream! _____

SOMETHING GOOD

Lyrics and Music by
RICHARD RODGERS

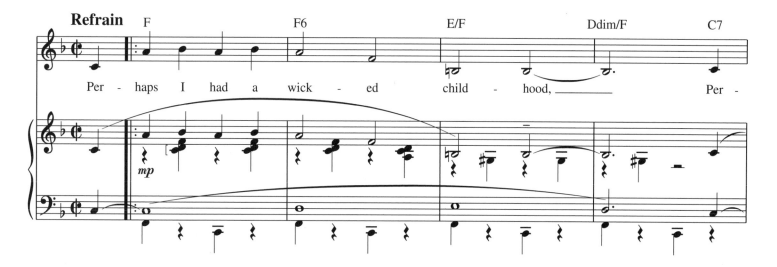

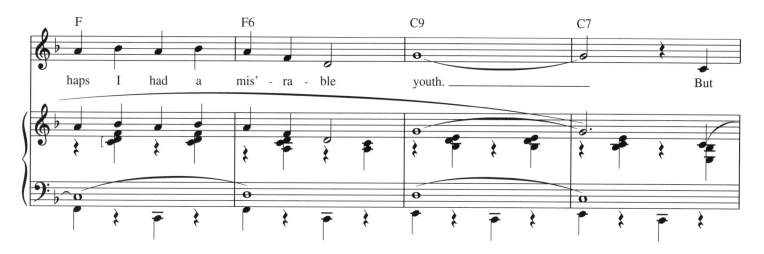

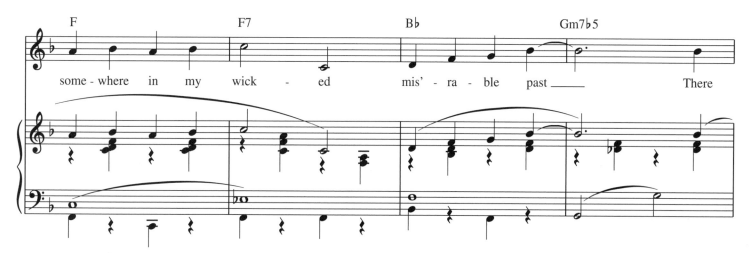

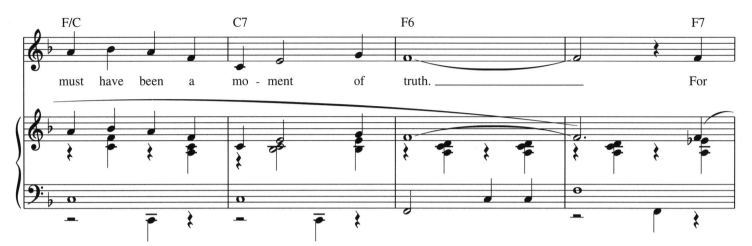

must have been a mo - ment of truth. _____ For

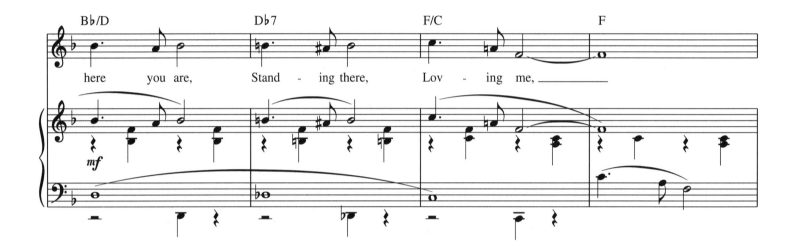

here you are, Stand - ing there, Lov - ing me, _____

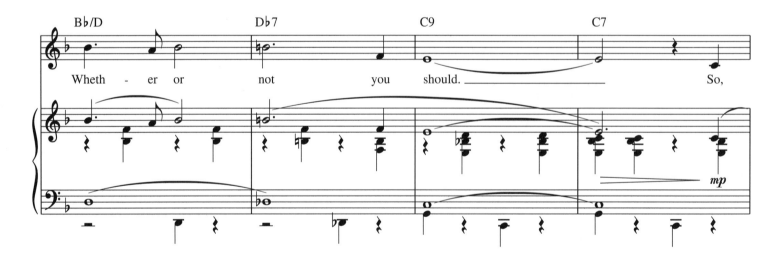

Wheth - er or not you should. _____ So,

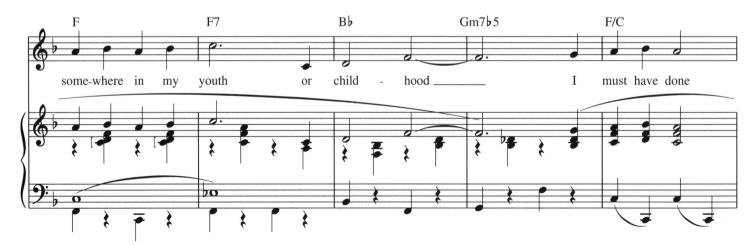

some-where in my youth or child - hood _____ I must have done

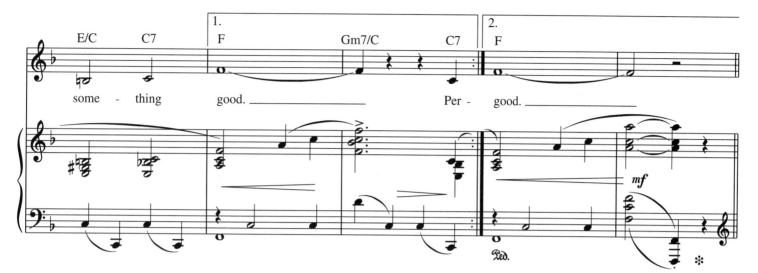

some - thing good. _____ Per - good. _____

Coda

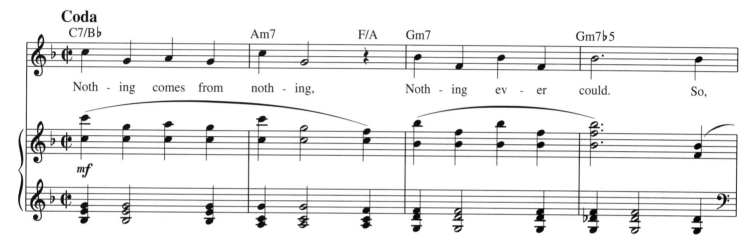

Noth - ing comes from noth - ing, Noth - ing ev - er could. So,

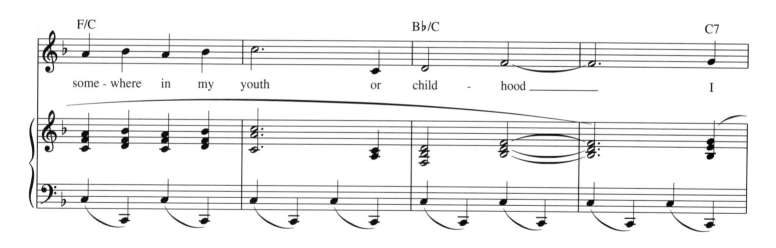

some - where in my youth or child - hood _____ I

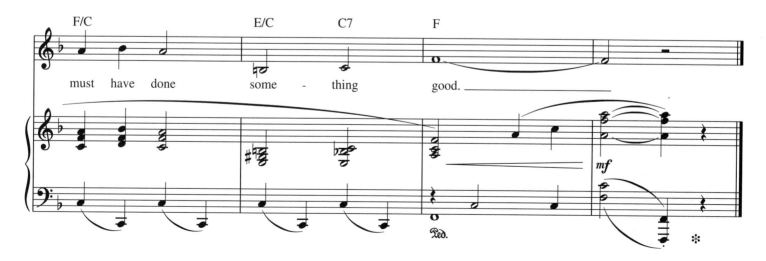

must have done some - thing good. _____

THE LONELY GOATHERD

Lyrics by OSCAR HAMMERSTEIN II
Music by RICHARD RODGERS

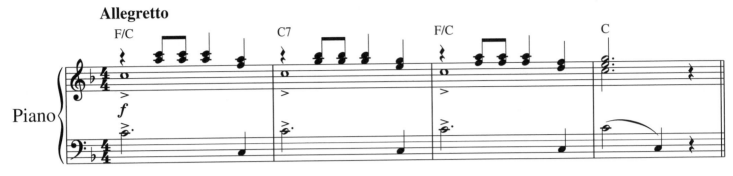

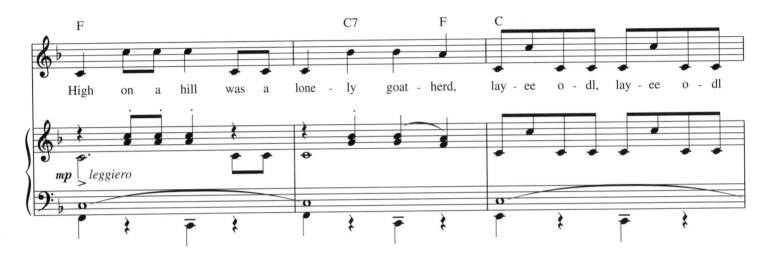

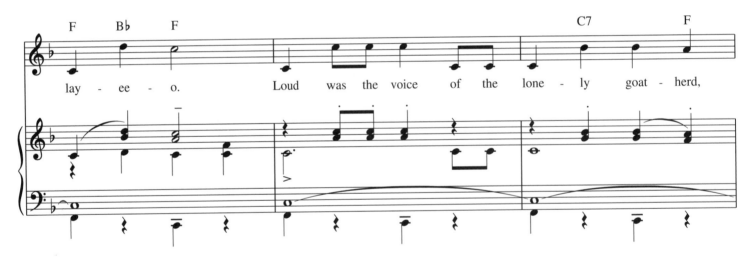

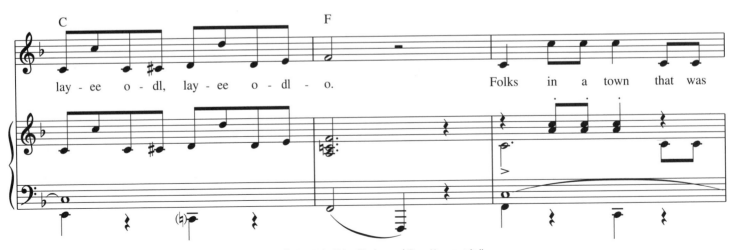

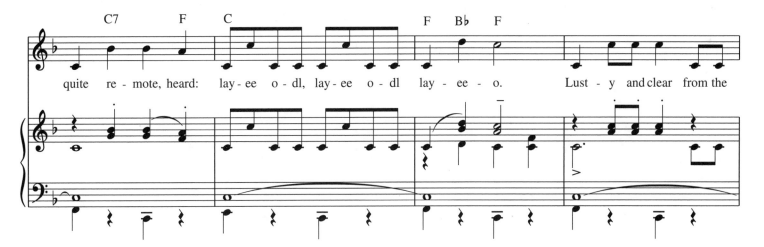

quite re - mote, heard: lay - ee o - dl, lay - ee o - dl lay - ee o. Lust - y and clear from the

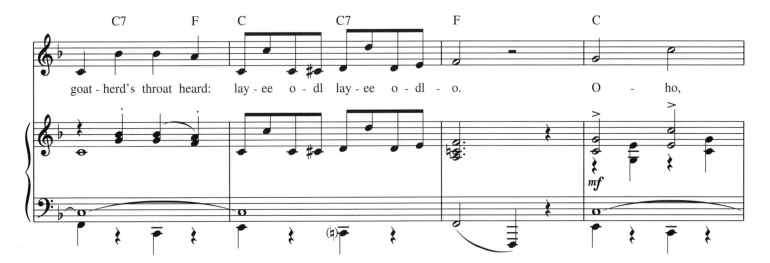

goat - herd's throat heard: lay - ee o - dl lay - ee o - dl - o. O - ho,

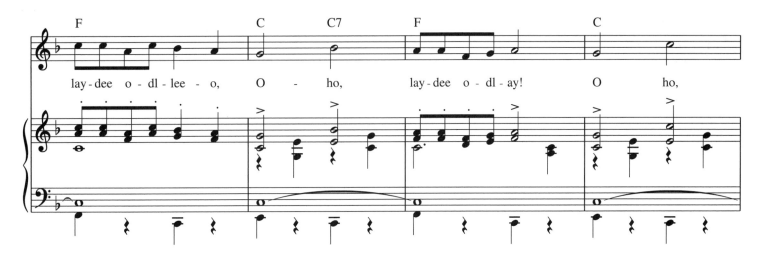

lay - dee o - dl - lee - o, O - ho, lay - dee o - dl - ay! O ho,

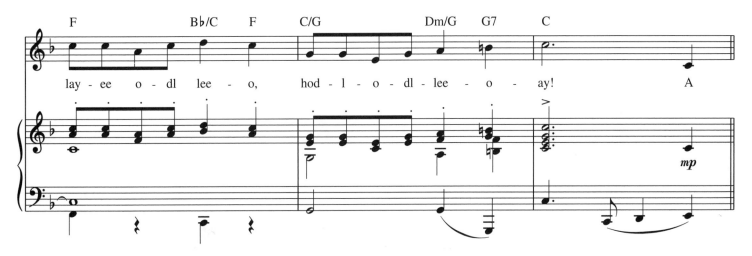

lay - ee o - dl lee - o, hod - l - o - dl - lee - o - ay! A

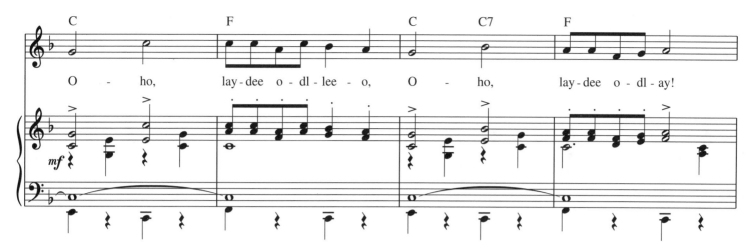

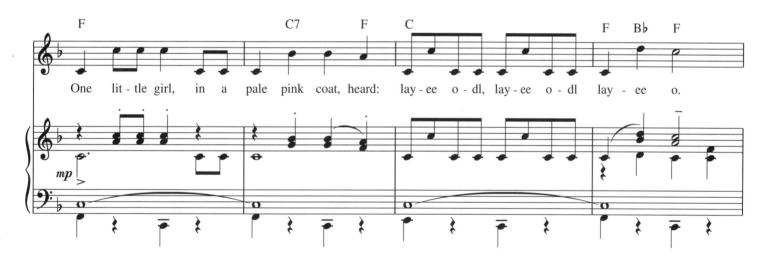

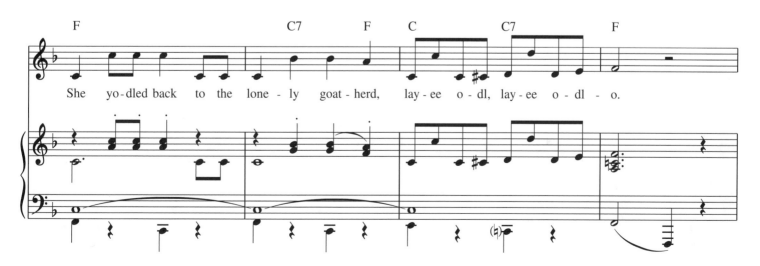

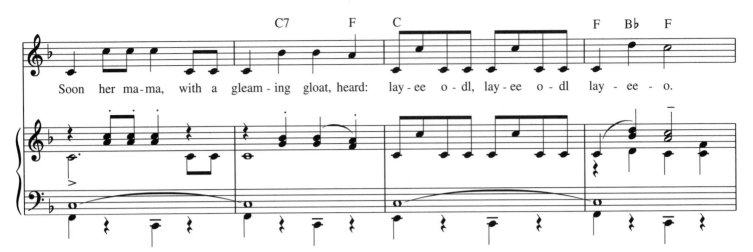

Soon her ma-ma, with a gleam-ing gloat, heard: lay-ee o-dl, lay-ee o-dl lay-ee-o.

What a du-et for a girl and goat-herd: lay-ee o-dl, lay-ee o-dl-o.

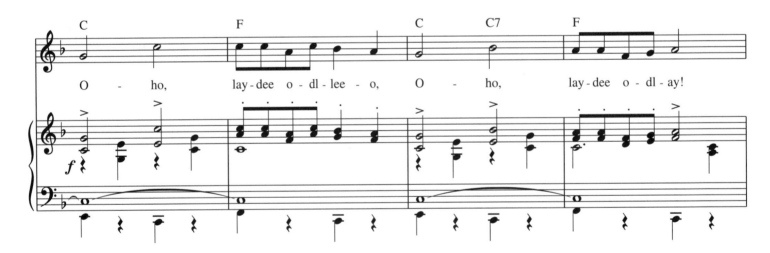

O - ho, lay-dee o-dl-lee-o, O - ho, lay-dee o-dl-ay!

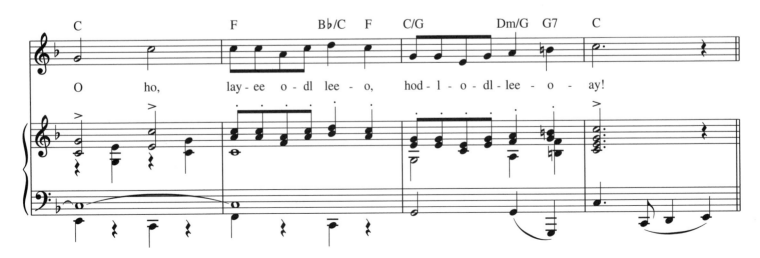

O ho, lay-ee o-dl lee-o, hod-l-o-dl-lee-o-ay!

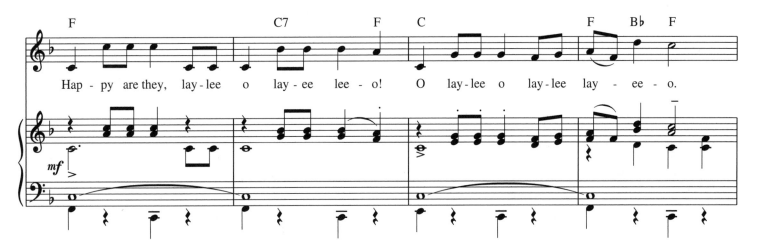

Hap - py are they, lay - lee o lay - ee lee - o! O lay - lee o lay - lee lay - ee - o.

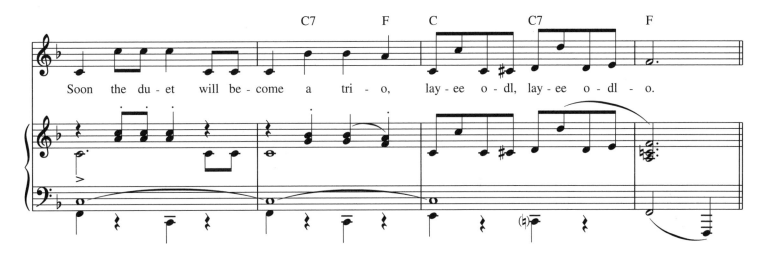

Soon the du - et will be - come a tri - o, lay - ee o - dl, lay - ee o - dl - o.

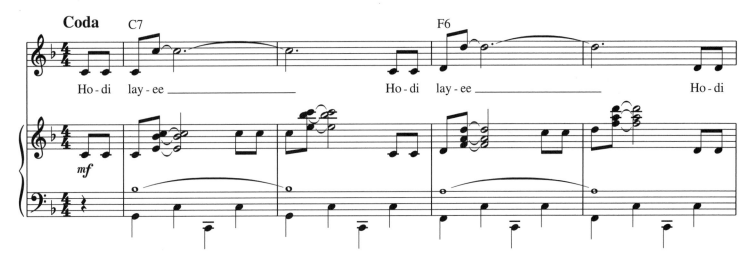

Coda

Ho - di lay - ee _____ Ho - di lay - ee _____ Ho - di

lay - ee _____ O - de lay - ee o - dl lee - e o - dl lay.

EDELWEISS

Lyrics by OSCAR HAMMERSTEIN II
Music by RICHARD RODGERS

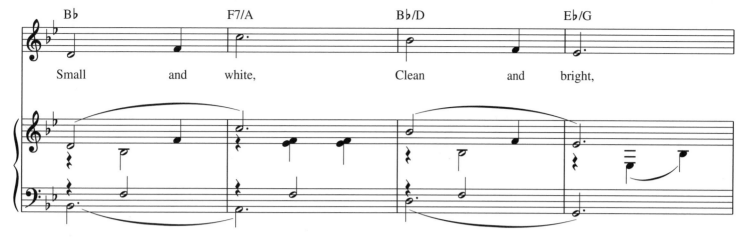

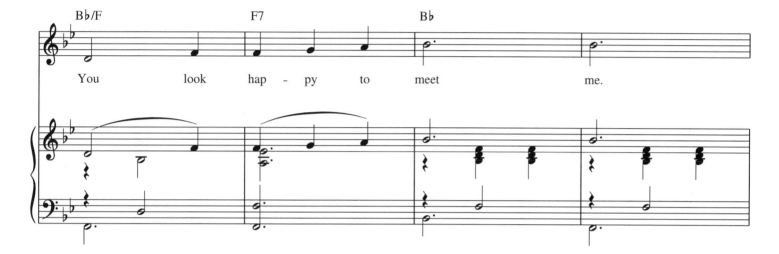

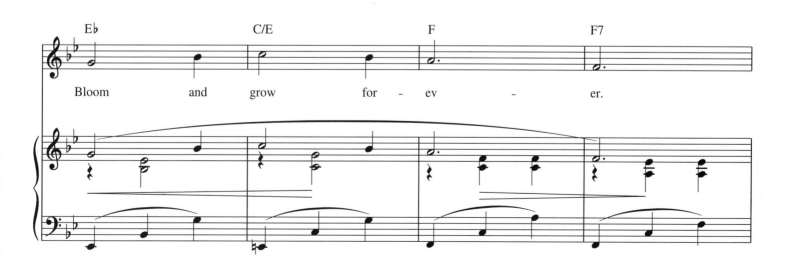

E - del - weiss, E - del - weiss,

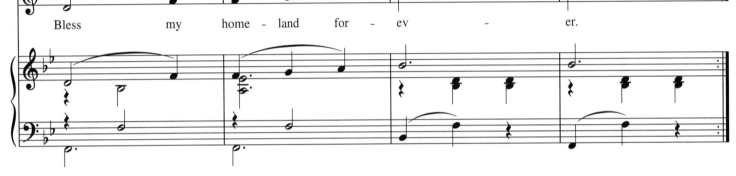

Bless my home - land for - ev - er.

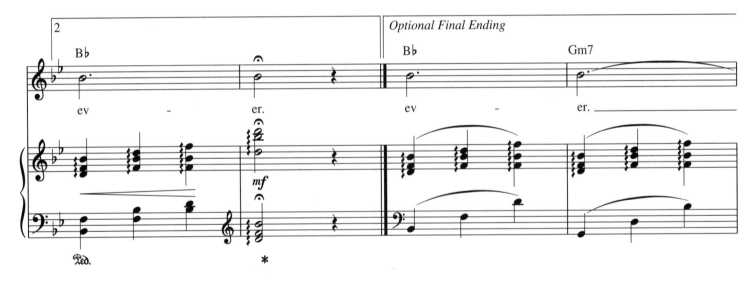

ev - er. ev - er.

Optional Final Ending

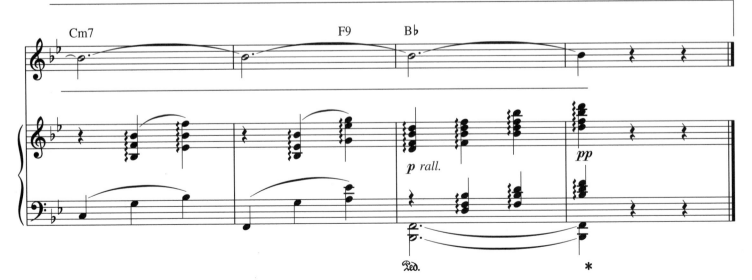